coastal
modern

coas
mo

sophisticated homes inspired by the ocean

tal dern

TIM CLARKE
with Jake Townsend

photographs by NOAH WEBB

clarkson potter/publishers
NEW YORK

Published in the United States by Clarkson Potter/Publishers, an imprint of the Crown Publishing Group, a division of Random House, Inc., New York.

www.crownpublishing.com

www.clarksonpotter.com

CLARKSON POTTER is a trademark and POTTER with colophon is a registered trademark of Random House, Inc.

Library of Congress Cataloging-in-Publication Data

Clarke, Tim (Tim Dowd)
    Coastal modern : sophisticated homes inspired by the ocean / Tim Clarke. — 1st ed.
        p.   cm.
1. Clarke, Tim (Tim Dowd)—Themes, motives.   2. Interior decoration—United States.   3. Seaside architecture—United States.   I. Title.
II. Title: Sophisticated homes inspired by the ocean.
    NK2004.3.C59A4   2012
    747.092—dc22   2011015784

ISBN 978-0-307-71878-5

Printed in Hong Kong

Book interior and jacket design by Stephanie Huntwork

Book interior and jacket photography by Noah Webb

10 9 8 7 6 5 4 3

First Edition

FOR MY PARTNER-IN-LIFE,
ART LUNA,
without whose love, support,
and constant encouragement
this book would not have been
possible. You push me to be the
best that I can be. I love you.

INTRODUCTION

THERE IS SOMETHING simply magnetic about the ocean. For anyone who has felt its pull, the sea is a means of transport, a source of food, a place of joy and solace, as well as the backdrop for countless summers where memories of youth and age intertwine in the fabric of our lives.

Homes located on the ocean capture the imagination, for they embody the depth of feeling people hold for the sea. The beach house is more than just a place to live—it is a symbol of a life well lived. It is a refuge and a respite from life's grind, a paean to beauty and relaxation, and a celebration of both solitude and togetherness.

I design homes that embody a dream. From my first residential project onward, I set forth to create interior spaces that celebrate the freedom, lightness, and relaxed elegance of the perfect beach house regardless of the architectural style or location of the home.

I've been lucky enough to work with people who have trusted me and my team to make transformations on a very large architectural scale, often designing entire homes, and sometimes entire lifestyles, for them to feel renewed, refreshed, and reborn. Though it may sound rather over the top, I feel privileged to have witnessed the power beach house design has to change people's lives.

For far too long, modern design and architecture conveyed a cold and uncomfortable mood, and modern homes became caricatures of themselves: uninviting, uncompromising rooms that may have looked sleek and sexy but weren't places where you wanted to live your life. When people came to me looking for designs for their beachfront homes, which were often their second or even third residences, they wanted to get away from the showcases they lived in during the week and settle into something comfortable and real, without sacrificing style. So I began to create homes that embodied this relaxed way of living, and with each beach house, this theme began to shape itself into a more cohesive approach to design that I call coastal modern.

Filling a room with a variety of textures is essential in creating harmony.

Whether you live in Santa Monica or St. Louis, you can have a beach-inspired house—any living space can be transformed to embody the spirit of a coastal residence. Coastal modern is really a way of thinking, of looking at each space so that the home can be livable, but still truly modern. It should provide a break from the stresses of fast-paced lifestyles and serves as an oasis that fosters a feeling of closeness and warmth. The people I work with live all over the world, and many are hundreds of miles from the closest sand dune, but they come to me to help them create residences imbued with the essence of the sand and the sea and the magical interplay between the two. Even if you live in a noncoastal area, you can open your home to the outdoors to enhance the connection between indoors and outdoors and to reinforce the idea of an "imagined" coast.

Every home you see in this book embodies the coastal modern aesthetic, but the expression of this aesthetic is as varied as the homeowners themselves. There is no single design style, era, color scheme, size, or shape that typifies coastal modern, because the style is about a way of living and a way of looking at the world.

I've organized this book into five distinct styles of design that I have dubbed "Scandia surf," "seaside Mediterranean," "beach classic," "inherited ease," and "native woods." Moreover, the book flows according to the changing light of a day: starting from the palest and lightest residences of Scandia surf and seaside Mediterranean, moving into the bright midday of beach classic, and slowly approaching sunset with inherited ease and native woods. Each of these styles is an entirely unique way of approaching beach house design, and perhaps you will find ideas for your own living spaces.

I truly love what I do, and strive to create homes that inspire comfort, creativity, and passion. I hope the interiors in this book encourage you to create your own perfect beach house; one that both embodies who you are, and who you hope to be.

OPPOSITE With inspiring views like this, adornment is unnecessary. Simple furnishings with clean, unbroken lines enhance the seascape.

FOLLOWING PAGE, LEFT The pale yellow-orange in these outdoor umbrellas take inspiration from the orange tones in the boulders below.

FOLLOWING PAGE, RIGHT Small design moments tell big stories. Don't forget to fill in the blanks.

coastal modern basics

ALL COASTAL MODERN HOMES FIND inspiration in the basic foundation described in this chapter, but each home is also unique. No matter how fast paced, chaotic, or successful a life is, there always seems to be a feeling that things could be better, different, more beautiful, less fussy, smaller, bigger, lighter, darker. What works for one person often doesn't work for another—but that is the point of design. It's completely personal, utterly unique, and should reflect who you truly are or want to be—certainly not who or what someone else wants you to be.

foundations for a style

WHEN I WAS given the chance to design my first coastal home, I realized that I could use my belief in freedom, my love of an elegant but relaxed home, and, finally, of a house that fosters a life lived rather than a life performed, to create interiors that would change people. I threw out the old conventions that dictated stuffy, overdone interiors that felt as if you were being ushered out the moment you walked in. Instead I created homes with soaring spaces, a mix of carefully chosen old furnishings balanced with new accessories and the use of colors, textures, and fabrics that referenced the home's natural surroundings.

I try to avoid shapes, colors, and textures that oppose serenity. Though I love modern and contemporary furnishings, objects, and architecture, a coastal modern home is about celebrating nature, not opposing it. Modernism and postmodernism are, in part, a celebration of the industrial revolution, and they strive to place humankind in context with an automated age. Coastal modern is meant to find a balance between mechanization and nature. Furnishings should still have those crisp lines inspired by the machine age but should be constructed of untreated, unpainted materials like wood and stone that reveal their true nature. With these new pieces, I always mix in things carefully selected at flea markets, tag sales, and local antiques shops. Not only do these used items convey a sense of life, but they are the ultimate in sustainable design: it's recycling at its most efficient. Lastly, color schemes reflect those that you find in coastal areas around the world. Colors of sand, sky, water, and planet—even the surrounding soils—inspire the palette.

OPPOSITE Warm and cool; rough and smooth; modern and classic; rooms that achieve balance with opposing elements are rooms that work.

OPENING PAGE This home, located on the coast in the Pacific Northwest, sits above a roiling, dramatic sea and beneath oft-cloudy skies. Reflective elements like this gold-leaf branch table and the metalized linen pillow refract light on cloudy days.

PRECEDING PAGE, LEFT Driftwood, shells, and that gray-green light you only find on the coast during winter can inspire a color palette for a room.

PRECEDING PAGE, RIGHT This arresting seascape ignites passion in a bathroom.

FOLLOWING PAGE, LEFT Soft textiles in warm, neutral tones coupled with walls of glass that positively flood the room with light make for a modern, comfortable, and very coastal-inspired space.

FOLLOWING PAGE, RIGHT The presence of water, whether natural or from a man-made source, encourages an inherent tranquillity, and often provides inspiration for interior color schemes. Pools like this bend, refract, and diffuse sunlight throughout the interior of the home, bringing rooms to life with color and light.

LEFT This kitchen is layered with crisp shades and textures. Though light dances across the surface of the glazed tile backsplash and the gleaming stainless steel of the fixtures, the rubbed-oak island brings the focus to the center, where all of the action is. The elegance of this project even pervades the kitchen, which features silver chandeliers chosen for the candlestick-like appearance.

FOLLOWING PAGE Collections of objects, no matter their provenance, add life to rooms. Here, glass pieces of differing sizes reflect the dazzling mottled sunlight that bounces off of the surface of a nearby pool.

keep it simple

THE BENEFIT OF coastal modern design is that it's an accessible approach to creating sustainable environments. Rather than requiring large-scale changes, coastal modern homes embody the basic tenet of the environmental movement: thinking globally by acting locally. I acquire furnishings and objects from local sources, including artisans and craftspeople. I favor custom-made pieces over mass-produced ones, and I use heirloom and antique furnishings whenever possible. Simplicity is demanding, and creating minimalist interiors does not mean doing as little as possible. Such a well-thought-out minimal room often works because enough space is left between objects and furniture to create a sense of symmetry.

The natural tendency of anyone who is ready to make a change is to throw everything out the door, even down to the architecture, and to start from scratch, but only the most dire of design disasters requires a total makeover: with many houses built in the last thirty years, the main issue is one of overdesign and clutter. Coastal modern is the opposite; these homes use only what is necessary, useful, and lovely to live with.

I once met with a couple who owned a large showcase house right on the water. This was a highly coveted residence, situated in a community that has seen its share of teardowns and developments erected in place of those charming cottages that initially drew admirers to the area. A previous decorator had told them that the solution to their needs was akin to tearing the home apart, including ripping off the entire roof, and starting from scratch and bare studs. I disagreed—this isn't always the right decision when you can find other ways to create a dream home without completely starting over. Sometimes the best solution is to pare down and simplify a space. It's easy to look at homes built in faddish periods—seventies and eighties

Scale becomes more vertical when accentuated by a series of arches. The eye is instantly drawn to the moody landscape at the end of this corridor.

houses are great examples—and simply dismiss them as design mistakes. The *Brady Bunch* house, with its open staircase, orange kitchen counters, and heavy woods, is the prototypical example. At the time, it exemplified the height of suburban modern and was the envy of the fictional neighborhood. A decade later, of course, it looked as painfully and cartoonishly outdated as a polyester leisure suit. Twenty years after that, the house was "cool" again and would have been used as a backdrop for a fashion ad; five years after that, it was "ugly" again. Tastes change: there are no absolutes in design, and rarely are there situations where the bones of the house are so outmoded that they need to be discarded entirely.

Homes built in the 1980s—those ubiquitous, nonsdescript drywall boxes—offer great examples of beneficial design elements that can be worked with. There are often bathrooms for every bedroom, with large, efficient kitchens and expansive living rooms. (Remember, you had to have a place for all of that overstuffed furniture and room for your shoulder pads and big hair.) They only need a little added detail and pleasing decoration to be successful.

Simplicity applies to architecture as well. I much prefer efficient and practical bedrooms and bathrooms designed on a smaller scale, leaving more space for large public areas such as kitchens, dining rooms, and living rooms. Bedrooms are for sleeping—after all, you spend most of your bedroom time in the dark, or with your eyes closed. The sleeping spaces are, of course, well appointed and comfortable, but there is no reason to create little apartments designed to encourage solitude. I like to design large, open living spaces for entertaining that encourage people to spend time together instead of hiding away in the bedroom.

This home has a strong sense of place. The subtle glass and stone forms feel as if they might have organically grown from the earth itself.

LEFT Though this room may appear to be monochromatic, it is the subtle layering of soft hues and naturally inspired textures and patterns that create a warm and inviting space.

FOLLOWING PAGE, RIGHT This well-proportioned and airy bedroom is coastal modern style at its best: restraint and purity are always paramount when layering.

Though most of this home echoes the neutral, brooding palette of the Pacific Northwest coastal region, moments of color are key to a balanced room.

naturally inspired

DESIGN SHOULD REFLECT NATURE. Color, texture, and pattern on your walls, floors, furnishings, and objects will make more sense when they directly reference the inspiring natural palette that surrounds you. When you're living at the beach, the shells, the sand, the sky, and the weather are the elements that provide a gorgeous palette. In other settings, such as in the city, your color scheme can reflect either an aspirational palette, using lots of vibrant, naturally found colors to give the impression of nature, or you can use the colors of the urban environment to bring the outside in.

A city may look bleak, but if you look closely, it too is alive with nature. Think about the views; what can be seen outside the window is like a painting. The quality of light that is reflected back into the room depends a lot on the colors you choose. I'm often inspired by reflections of concrete, reflections of lush green, reflections of sand or water—these all provide points of reference for color palettes. One of my previous homes was a contemporary industrial-style loft located just a few blocks from one of the most popular beaches in the world, where my view was mostly sky. Though interior materials included cinder block, steel railings, and exposed heating and plumbing systems, I created living spaces that were warm, cozy, contemporary, chic, and completely modern by adding personal objects and wooden furnishings to the raw space. The colors I chose were mostly pale, as I didn't want to detract from the wonderful vibrancy of the blue sky views. You can have the city at the beach, the beach in the city, or any combination thereof—coastal modern works no matter where you are.

Both form and function come from the natural environment. It's so easy to forget that our manufactured world, with its artificial patinas, is mostly derived from nature, and one would be hard pressed to find some color, line, or pattern that does not already exist in nature. Here, grasses of various types are used as design elements in this contemporary home.

soak it in

WHEN APPROACHING A PROJECT, I begin with the unseen. Perhaps this sounds a bit esoteric when I'm talking about a discipline that is devoted entirely to what is experienced visually and tactilely. But before I gather color palettes, swatches, themes, and visual references, I need to first understand a place through the lens of my five senses. The true power of a home lies in what you experience subconsciously when you enter its space.

I begin by soaking in the essence of the property, often visiting construction sites alone and wandering about with a small notebook and my camera. I'll snap informal pictures of the natural environment, taking notes on aspects of the land that pique my senses.

As an experiment, leave your cell phone, your music, your work, and your distractions behind you and simply take a walk outside of your home or look out the windows. Notice the way that nature arranges color patterns, layers textures, and mixes symmetry and asymmetry in the shapes of all things. Even if you live in a city, where trees and grass fight with concrete and steel for space, these same principles hold true. You'll be astounded at the perfection of design created by the ultimate designer: Mother Earth.

What is interesting about this simple exercise is that it also helps you create a cohesive picture of your design project in your mind's eye. When you're creating a home that reflects who you are, you need to take the time to get to know who you are. This may sound like a casual aphorism, but knowing who you are is a lifetime pursuit. Your changing view of yourself and the way you want to live should be constantly updated in the design of your home. Most design-conscious people, in fact, do this instinctively, changing their homes whenever they feel that indescribable urge to transform or evolve.

The porthole in the ceiling looks into the pool one floor above (also shown on page 111). The small river stones coupled with the nautical shape of the window give the subterranean room a shiplike feel.

LEFT Handmade objects, like these French bird sculptures, when coupled with the *faux bois*–framed mirror, keep this stately home from taking itself too seriously.

FOLLOWING PAGE, RIGHT Natural unbleached linen covers the blocklike forms of these simple chairs.

Laguna Beach, at the height of
summer. The absolute riot of colors
nature has provided for this palette
is breathtaking.

scandia

surf

the new Nordic style at the beach

2

THERE ARE FEW CONTEMPORARY
cultures whose design embraces order,
simplicity, and stark beauty like that of the
Scandinavians. When one pictures Scandinavian
design, often flat-pack furniture or the Danish
modern movement springs to mind; each is
equally indicative of this style. Furnishings
produced in Scandinavia are clean, well-
proportioned, and functional without being
expensive, fussy, or unnecessarily adorned.
Such design is the opposite of baroque; it's
stylish without relying on fashion, and it
never fights for attention in a room. The light
and airy aesthetic of Scandinavian design is
effective in counteracting the darkness that
pervades the Nordic winters. In short, it's a
style that's in perfect form for a beach house.

Scandia surf style mixes a modern
aesthetic with antiques, illustrated
here in this presentation of an aged
Gustavian chest at the end of a
light-filled hall.

the quest for light

HOMES THAT I CALL SCANDIA SURF embody the best of the
Scandinavian aesthetic in their look and feel. The style is understated
in both form and palette, taking inspiration from the wind- and
sea-battered homes of the Nordic coastlines that withstand an almost
constant barrage of salt spray year-round. The exterior paint, often in
muted blues, grays, and whites, has a weathered, lasting patina that
reveals the harsh beauty of this part of the world.

The cultures of Sweden, Norway, and Denmark emphasize
frugality, pragmatism, and self-sufficiency, and this shows in the
way they design their homes. Objects and furnishings are not purely
decorative but made to last, no matter the changing tides of fashion
and trend. Danish modern pieces from the twentieth century look
sublimely at home in a contemporary residence; the clean lines and
timeless materials never go out of style.

Natural resources are of utmost concern in a Scandia surf
home. Like the Nordic cultures that inspired them, these homes make
as much use of local materials as possible. Nordic people often draw
their livelihoods from the natural environment and see themselves as
stewards of it. The use of local wood and stone is a necessity and has
the added benefit of creating an intangible aesthetic connecting the
interior and the natural environs.

Scandinavian homes are elegantly proportioned and
symmetrical and feature classical detailing—pulling from the best of
European architecture but paring it down to its most basic and efficient
elements. Quiet in both color and texture, these homes make use of
large systems of windows and strategic mirrors so as to maximize light
and minimize shadows and darkness.

OPPOSITE Scandia surf bathrooms
are always simple and spare.
This master bath is an exercise
in informed restraint. The
handsome view is treated as if
it were a painting; the board-
formed concrete wall is an elegant
treatment that doesn't detract from
the experience.

FOLLOWING PAGES The bold vertical
stripes are a modern interpretation
of the soaring forests seen in all
directions from this room.

The earth tones chosen for
the custom-made upholstered
headboard and woven pillow
take inspiration from the eroded
coastline just at the perimeter of
the residence.

The IKEA bureau proves that functional, affordable pieces can make great additions to a space, especially when personalized with collections of one-of-a-kind pieces.

ABOVE This purple chair found its inspiration in the otherworldly fields of purple flora that surround this magical cliff-side home.

FOLLOWING PAGE, LEFT There are no rules. These delicately detailed mirrors hanging in front of the windows allow filtered light to flood the bathroom while creating focal points above these twin sinks. Carefully chosen flea market finds, like these brass cranes, take the place of visually unappealing personal grooming items.

FOLLOWING PAGE, RIGHT Antique French encaustic tiles, used in a bathroom, echo the deep forest hues and subtle colors of winter skies.

A beach home needn't be overstuffed, overdecorated, or oversaturated: this under-the-stairs collection of art includes both local and well-known artists, cheap flea market finds, and machine parts. The secret is in the simple mix.

minimal details, simple forms

SCANDINAVIAN DESIGN HAS been so influential on contemporary interiors because not only is this style light, breezy, and easy to incorporate, but also it works in concert with the natural world.

Gray serves as the best foundation for a color palette accented with the lightness of blue, pale yellow, and blushy pink because it is easier on the eyes than white, especially on blindingly sunny days or in the glaring fog—conditions that coastal homes often see. The ceilings are important in this palette as well and should receive as much attention as other planes. They are often detailed with wood beams, tongue-and-groove work, paneling, or wallpaper. The floors might be painted driftwood gray or bleached free of all color and left to look more natural. The minimal details and simple forms of the decor are best placed on unvarnished wood floors, and the furniture is slightly worn, or at least covered in fabrics that age well.

Fabric is mostly solid in color and made of natural materials. Curtains should feature blown-up abstract patterns that are hand-blocked on natural linen. I love using faded ticking stripe on furniture as it gives a space a muted whimsy that lightens dark wintry days. I look for rugs that are woven "sweater" wool, or jute and wool that have been woven together for softness and durability, and for grid, plaid, or stripe patterns. I upholster furnishings to also be simple and functional with almost no detail, using mostly natural linen.

Scandia surf style features open storage, and therefore these homes must be neat, clean, and orderly. Such an open plan facilitates visual organization and saves time and effort—eliminating the need to hunt through cupboards and drawers. These homes are sensibly arranged; they are useful and full of life and purpose.

A successfully designed Scandia surf home uses colors and forms that echo the natural environment. This office space feels at once relaxed and sophisticated without overpowering the senses. Furnishings and accent pieces in blond wood work together with driftwood-inspired lamps and side tables to give the room a sun-bleached timelessness that typifies beach house life. Roman shades in a pattern that you might find in an English country home lend an air of sophistication, while the sea foam colors of the upholstered furniture and striped rug are immediately associated with the sea. The Moroccan-style leather ottoman brings a subtle ethnic element into the design scheme.

Spots of watery turquoise inspired by the ocean are the main colors in this dining room.

The modern interpretation of the ladder-back chair provides sculptural punctuation to an otherwise white space.

ABOVE A pantry featuring shelving filled with lovely dishware is as effective as a piece of sculpture and decidedly more functional. The baskets are handmade by local Native American artisans.

RIGHT An open kitchen creates flow in the home.

FOLLOWING PAGE, LEFT This salt marsh is located on the opposite side of the property—away from the beach. The interplay of color here, most notably the reds, oranges, and browns, inspired much of the palette in the home.

FOLLOWING PAGE, RIGHT Coastal modern homes mix old and new to create a feeling of lived-in luxury. This antique Gustavian cabinet in its original paint is functional as well as beautiful. Located in the dining room, it houses the placemats and napkins to make setting the table easy—at a moment's notice.

This outdoor room feels like a living room. The contemporary outdoor furnishings could do double duty in any indoor space. The wood carving nestled in the surrounding shrubbery rounds out the feeling of a private secret garden.

sandyland cove

Treating outdoor living spaces with as much importance as the indoors is part of a well-designed coastal home. This outdoor "living room" was painted in the same family of gray found throughout the indoor spaces, but the shade is slightly more saturated. Colors used outdoors should be within the same palette as your indoor scheme but more intense, as they must compete with the sunlight. These modern, simple wooden furnishings are offset by bold striping that feels almost like something you would see on the beach in St. Tropez. I intentionally used horizontal stripes on the couch and chairs to play off the vertical details on the exterior structure. Always have some opposition in a space; even if it isn't immediately noticed, it creates an emotional experience.

A BREATHTAKING LOCATION provided instant inspiration for this beach house remodel. Situated just a few miles south of Santa Barbara, California, this oceanfront home sits on one of the most sought-after beaches in the area. Families that own homes here rarely put them up for sale, making any residence that comes onto the market a coveted item. When the family purchased the property, they were planning on spending summers there, though their primary residence is just up the coast and also very close to the beach.

Even before work had begun on the remodel, my initial visit to the home provided a wealth of ideas. Though the house and its surrounding property sit just a hundred feet from the sand, its relationship to the changing tides and oceanfront weather is immediate. Perhaps most striking is the dramatic play between the ocean on one side and a protected salt marsh on the other. Viewed from the living room, the ruddy, ever-changing, chaparral-covered mountain range plays in visual concert with the crashing waves just beyond the expanse of grass outside. This home is truly at one with the nature that surrounds it, and it was my paramount concern to make that relationship an integral part of the design scheme. I knew immediately that the home was well suited for the breezy lightness that typifies the Scandia surf style.

I spent several days walking the property, experiencing changes in weather, light, and temperature so that I could seamlessly weave the character of the land into the design. This holistic approach allowed the home and its surroundings to reveal their unique character to me, resulting in unexpected inspiration and design direction.

At SandyLand, color revealed itself to me first: the sandy beach tones were broken by the dramatic tar-covered rocks that cut the coastline like giant chips of coal. This theatrical play between light and dark is reflected in many of the color choices throughout the home, including the rustic weathered charcoal gray floors and in the choice of artwork throughout. These rich, dark, natural elements when

coupled with light tones inspired by the beach are very much in step with the coastal homes found in Scandinavia, where an inky layer of pine tar protects them from the elements.

The bulk of the home reflects a muted, monochromatic color scheme. The dominant hues are pale and matte, only occasionally broken up by dramatic splashes of orange—another color inspired by the surrounding natural environment. In the first few days spent on the property, I noticed how the oranges and reds of the mountain foliage worked in concert with the muted, more subtle coral hues on the underside of shells found littered along the beach. The use of color as derived from the natural environment may not readily create immediate connections to the surrounding area, but it ends up subliminally connecting the interior spaces to the natural world around the home. The people I design for often describe feeling instantly comfortable but cannot immediately explain why; often I find that these subtle references to the natural world are the cause.

The use of either recycled or local materials is an important part of the Scandia surf aesthetic, and we used such materials readily throughout this residence. For SandyLand Cove, I used locally sourced items, including a collection of unfired Bauer pottery and small sea-inspired objects made of shell and other naturally derived materials to incorporate the local culture into the scheme as much as possible. Using materials of this nature also created subliminal comfort in the family and guests, as the design subtly referenced the world just outside the door.

The interplay of nature and architecture is truly magical at SandyLand Cove and reminds me of those timeless coastal homes in Norway, Sweden, and Denmark. The natural setting, coupled with an ever-changing microclimate, creates a unique set of needs that makes for a truly special residence.

The kitchen has an expansive plan and looks out into the rest of the house. Open kitchens are my preferred style when creating a beach home—they foster lively conversation and a sense of togetherness. The frosted glass on the cabinets takes on the pale blue of the rest of the room. Though the stove and refrigerator are state of the art, the cabinets have a vintage, almost Cape Cod feel to them, which nicely offsets the cold steel of the fixtures.

RIGHT Though the lawn that leads up to the sea is vast, we decided to create this small intimate deck to tame the space. Sometimes smaller spaces have bigger impacts. Simple teak outdoor furniture and umbrellas in a neutral butter tone don't overpower the senses or distract from the incredible scenery.

FOLLOWING PAGE, LEFT Mix patterns, mix textures, mix periods—and don't get attached to perfection. Perfectionism destroys balance.

FOLLOWING PAGE, RIGHT Even the sunsets at SandyLand Cove provide inspiration. Note the bold oranges, yellows, and reds reflected in the ocean's surface and throughout the color scheme in the rest of the home.

mediter

seaside
ranean

the modern approach to *le style Provençal*

FOR ANYONE WHO HAS TRAVELED TO THE magical coastal towns along the Mediterranean Sea, the allure is positively magnetic. From Homer's *The Odyssey* onward, miles of pages and hours of screen time have celebrated this most special of coastal places. It is no wonder that American beach towns, especially those in California, where the climate is similar, have adopted architectural and design styles that draw inspiration from the Mediterranean. Seaside Mediterranean homes contain accents that echo the art, architecture, and design of France, Greece, Morocco, Italy, and Spain—but softly blended so the very essence of these special places is implied but never referenced directly.

simplicity and serenity

MY SEASIDE MEDITERRANEAN HOMES maintain an elegance and a purity that typifies homes near the Mediterranean. As with most designs, one always begins with the foundation, and in seaside Mediterranean homes that foundation is usually stone that looks as if it's pulled from a local quarry. I use soft, aged French limestone and Calcutta Crema marble in colors ranging from ecru and cream all the way to the gray of a deeply cloudy morning just before rain falls.

In some rooms, the floors feature weathered soft hardwoods salvaged from France's Bourgogne region. When coupled with a muted color palette, their warm base colors create a womblike interior space. Inspired by the saturated light of postcard-perfect seaside towns, Mediterranean homes on the ocean feature views that are composed almost entirely of sky and water, and hardly ever sand. Earthy interiors act as the balancing element in a concert of blues and greens.

I also use mosaic tile floors throughout, as these intricate, often unnoticed works of domestic art carry with them the spirit of ancient stone. When traveling along the Mediterranean coast, I noticed muted plaster walls anchored by intricate and ancient mosaic floors. My experience of such rooms was akin to stepping into an aesthetic time machine where the embrace of the past and the sense of familial warmth created a seductive atmosphere unlike anyplace I have ever been.

I use wood of many types liberally in these homes. When not made of stone, the floors are of wide-plank European oak, whose pale warmth and dry, open-grain textures give them the feeling of having been aged for generations by salt and sand. Windows are framed in mahogany that is bleached and stained to a warm taupe gray. Beams are made of reclaimed timber, and if I do use paint, I use matte, chalklike colors so that one element never overwhelms another.

OPPOSITE Seaside Mediterranean homes celebrate outdoor living, and eating is no exception. These chairs are inspired by vintage Hollywood director's chairs but have been updated and made practical for outdoor use with soft vinyl upholstery. The large sculptural succulent makes for a dramatic centerpiece.

OPENING PAGE This is the entrance to Rocky Point, a seaside Mediterranean home. Note the undeniable pull of this cozy courtyard. The rubble-like Lompoc stone with its thick grout and the red tile roof with its stacked edge make the house feel strong and lasting. The roof tiles are new but are a mixture of colors, so they feel worn with age. The stair risers are made of antique encaustic cement tile.

The integral-color plaster (plaster that has pigment added to the mix) that I prefer a natural stone color with a matte finish that seamlessly integrates with the rest of the design. Bullnose edge details are liberally employed throughout the architecture—in the countertops, the stairs, and the doorframes—so that edges are blurred and little attention is called to the transition from one room to the next.

Interiors in these homes are designed so that they are almost always flooded in natural, buttery sunlight. I use skylights and large-scale plate glass where possible and folding or sliding doors in rooms that open up to the outdoors. Color schemes are such that light is reflected and enhanced but rarely absorbed. Sunlight is another decorating tool, and the natural light that results is often the most commented-upon aspect of these homes. The dramatic interplay of light and shadow, coupled with as many seamless transitions from indoors to out, creates homes where nature is as much a part of everyday life as are the furnishings and decor.

RIGHT Hide your TV from view as is done here using bleached mahogany panels above the fireplace. The slightly rusted, painted iron chandelier is reminiscent of small flags rustling in the windswept square of a provincial coastal hamlet.

FOLLOWING PAGE, LEFT Non-flowering plants like this luscious succulent are often thought of as entirely green, but one look at this vibrant plant reveals a shocking pink hue that can be used as a layer of color in interiors.

There is no danger in mixing texture, pattern, and period—even in a seaside Mediterranean home. Colors are subtle and carefully used to inject just a moment of passion in this otherwise calm, oceanic space.

Art of the
Twentieth Century

1900, 1919
The Avant-garde
Movements

FRANK LLOYD WRIGHT

Silent Theater: The Art of Edward Hopper *Walter Wells*

RIGHT The layers of light are the key in this Laguna Beach living room. The exquisite antique carpet over the limestone floor serves as the foundation for this room.

FOLLOWING PAGE, RIGHT Seaside Mediterranean style is light, plain, pure, elegant, and discrete. This room is constantly bathed in natural light that streams through a large opening framing a seaside view.

faded by the
seaside sun

COLORS, LIKE THE FURNISHINGS, fixtures, and materials, should be of the "barely there" variety. Think linen, parchment, and twine as inspiration. Seaside Mediterranean homes depend as much on a tactile experience as they do on colors. A variety of textures on fabrics, walls, and floors are pleasing to the eyes when there is a marked lack of bold color. White should be tinted with hints of the muted color scheme. Blocklike shapes inspired by French decorating stand out against creamy plaster backdrops. This style is a modern approach to "Provençal" style—it is more spare, spacious, and consciously layered.

Rugs are important in seaside Mediterranean homes because of the muted aesthetic they can provide. I love antique Khotan rugs produced in eastern Turkestan in the eighteenth and nineteenth centuries. Their simple design, subdued colors, and lack of pile makes them a complement to this style.

Furniture in seaside Mediterranean homes is always European influenced, and the upholstery is traditionally shaped with bleached-wood legs. I use antique pieces from Italy or France, because the warm patinas contain the most complementary pale tones.

Fabrics are naturally dyed linens in solids but are mixed sparingly with large-scale prints. The designs might be ethnically inspired, but I love faded fabrics in which pattern is implied rather than overt. Materials include cotton, linen, and hemp—and even natural suede.

Above all, seaside Mediterranean homes exude a relaxed warmth and a strong, understated grandeur that is entirely unique. The warm, earthy tones coupled with solid, powerful foundational materials gives these homes an uncanny comfort that is at once contemporary and timeless.

Don't be afraid to layer in pale shades. Cream-colored linen curtains, napkins, and placemats as well as white upholstered chairs make this breakfast room positively glow.

LEFT This kitchen integrates nearly imperceptibly into the rest of the house by eschewing the obvious utilitarian elements found in most food preparation areas, and instead featuring a pared-down aesthetic. The countertops are mahogany, the cabinets are painted wood, and the floor is limestone.

FOLLOWING PAGE, LEFT A collection of ancient sand-cast tiles in the dining room have been mounted on linen and hung in a grid pattern.

FOLLOWING PAGE, RIGHT This dining room seems as if it could have been transported from a colonial mansion on Dominica, yet is simultaneously clean, modern, and up to date. Because of their casual mix of styles and periods, seaside Mediterranean homes always feel just right.

This headboard features upholstered linen with a surprising antique mirror inset that catches the light in the most unexpected of moments. Small artwork, including a framed collection of wax seals, give this room a personal touch.

rocky point

PERCHED ATOP A CLIFF in Palos Verdes, one of Southern California's oldest beach communities, the soaring, sweeping location of this home seems to maximize views of sun, sky, and surf with almost mathematical precision.

We were building from the ground up and had to follow a series of strict restraints as dictated by the building codes of Palos Verdes, which limited the size and design to a one-story home with a tile roof and exterior surfaces that incorporated stone and stucco. Driving through the community is an interesting—and singular—experience in that almost every home is designed according to some variation on this theme. The Mediterranean style is lovely and makes sense for the Southern California seaside climate, but what can be challenging is finding a way to create a home within these constraints that isn't rife with cliché. That said, this tightly controlled aesthetic actually provided a wealth of opportunity for using my seaside Mediterranean style.

I began the process as I always do, by taking a series of daily strolls around the empty site, through the surrounding neighborhood and along the beach. The views of crashing surf and endless blue skies are among the best I have ever seen, and the home sits high above the sand. It is this removed location that affords deeply affecting views of the ocean from almost every room in the home, though the owners' desire for an indoor/outdoor residence had to be balanced with the wind and cooler temperatures associated with it.

Though these design codes stipulate particular color schemes, they did not dictate whether the materials had to be new or old, or of a particular shade and hue. We used a type of red clay tile for the roof, mixing several shades to achieve the look of old tile. The muted colors gave the house a lived-in, authentic feeling. We coupled that with Lompoc stone in a rubble pattern and put an unusually large amount of grout between the stones to lend the exterior walls an air of history, which sets the tone for the interior experience.

An antique fireplace mantel anchors this outdoor room and negates the need for walls.

The couple was clear that they did not want a typical beach house filled with bright colors or a Mediterranean house in strong oranges or reds, but rather something more understated and suited to this dramatic location. The views are the real star here, and having anything too bright and splashy in the interior would take away from the experience.

I decided to go with a muted color palette based in part on Provençal architecture, but highly pared down to its most chalklike matte tones to prevent the rooms from feeling obvious and forced. I used bleached mahogany in warm taupe gray, like driftwood, on all the window casing and doors, which furthered the weathered, rich feeling of the interior spaces.

Built mostly of stone and plaster, the house looks as if it could have been constructed using materials pulled straight from the site, so it made sense to create an interior that felt as unobtrusive as possible. Natural woven linens and cottons in muted earth tones cover the furniture and upholstery. Italian and French antiques mix with Moroccan tables and objects that reference the sea. Of particular note are a metal chandelier that looks like coral and the collections of simple shells chosen for their sculptural quality that we placed throughout the home.

Interior details, including antique reclaimed beams, fireplaces, and plaster walls left in their natural state give this home the feeling of a long-lived life. The three antique French mantels in pale limestone in the bedroom, living room, and outdoors add a sense of history. Curtains in the living room and dining room hang in a natural linen fabric that has been hand-blocked with a muted, overall pattern that looks solid from a distance and as if it had been gently faded by the sun. In fact, the whole house feels this way: faded, loved, and lived in.

The master bedroom has one of the most dramatic and sweeping views in the house. To maximize this feature we intentionally kept the scale of the room on the larger side, with high ceilings and antique beams. The custom four-poster bed sits in the center and acts as a room within a room. The bedroom furniture has been painted with a pale milk paint so that it looks worn, simple, and useful.

RIGHT This kitchen feels as if it could have come from a cliffside home in Capri. We painted the cabinetry and fit the stove into what appears to be a hearth. This small detail gives the wall the appearance of having once been a fireplace used for cooking. All fixtures are in copper—not the usual nickel—which feels more European. A rough limestone lines all surfaces, and the center island is a stained mahogany butcher block in a warm, deep color.

FOLLOWING PAGE, LEFT Patterns and textures that find subtle inspiration in the cultures of the Mediterranean coasts are used throughout the home.

FOLLOWING PAGE, RIGHT The simple purity of design in this 1930s sofa in the style of Jean-Michel Frank injects an air of urban sophistication in an otherwise countrylike setting.

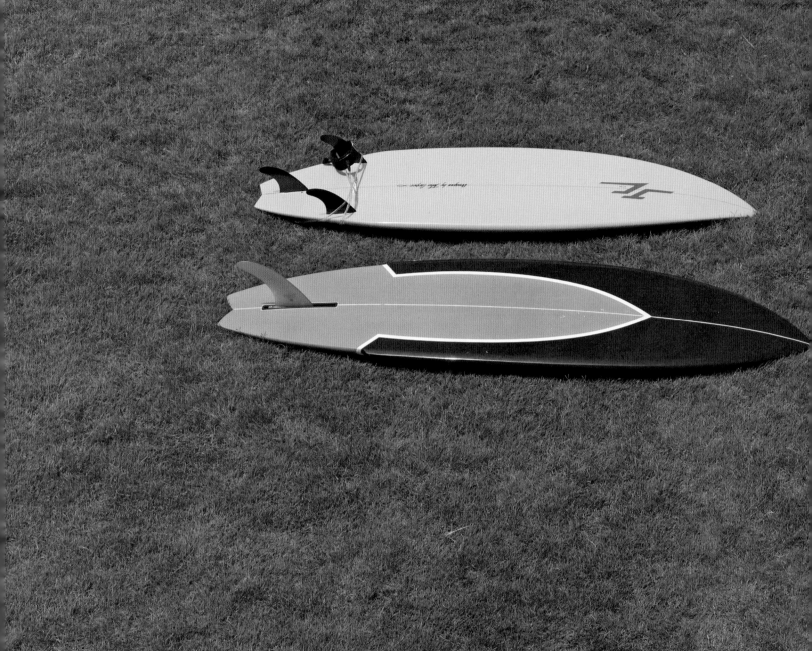

beach
classic

new American style

4

MUCH LIKE THE STYLE OF AMERICAN designers like Bill Blass, beach classic is timeless, yet modern and free of unnecessary embellishment—never dusty, cluttered, or out of touch. Beach classic homes possess the ebullient spirit of our nation, a zest for life and culture that encourages a sense of energy and optimism. At once firmly rooted in the past and completely contemporary, this aesthetic never goes out of fashion.

There is something intangible about American style—its essence is mercurial. America, a country of pride and ingenuity, stands for freedom and was built on a foundation of hard work and independence. The American people are what makes this country so special—and the design of my classic beach homes reflects this.

classic design
for everyday life

BEACH CLASSIC IS THE ESSENCE of a perfect New England life. Think back to the days when the Kennedy mansion at Hyannis Port was as much a part of the fabric of the American ideal as was the White House. We all remember the images of those bright, happy days when a large, successful American family laughed and roughhoused under the crisp New England sun. Those days gave Americans hope and embodied the possibility available to all of us. We imagined what it would be like to live in that lovely Cape Cod–style home, surrounded by a mixture of family heirlooms and furnishings that, while classic and elegant, were very much in everyday use.

Similarly, beach classic homes may be grand affairs upon first glance, soaring into the many thousands of square feet, but these living spaces are always comfortable, ordered, and scaled for the day to day. The design feels manageably human, and though intangible, you can sense this quality the moment you walk in the door. These elegant homes actually see use, wear, and life. Like a favorite pair of khakis that has been in the wardrobe for years, great classic design transcends fashion trends.

Furnishings may be traditional, giving homage to the past, but I upholster them in materials and patterns with a fresh, modern appeal. Beach classic homes focus on use and utility but never sacrifice style or comfort for high design. Furnishings and objects often feature natural materials—untreated cotton and denim, bleached woods, and raw metals—all of which create comfort and ease when you enter the spaces. Upholstery often consists of plain organic fabrics or simple, elegant, bold prints that resemble "weekend clothes"—polo shirts or your favorite sundress that makes you think of unfettered summer days spent in the warm sea breezes.

OPPOSITE Rooms that see heavy use, like this pool house, do well with furniture that performs double duty: these cabana striped couches convert to beds in a snap.

OPENING PAGE This study is layered in natural materials: bamboo, hemp, sea grass, and glass among them, giving it a comfortable, nautical feel that instantly transports.

East Coast country, rather than the Southern California beach, influences these homes. The kids, the dogs, and their neighborhood friends come and go as they please without being scolded. Beach classic is a mixture of the personal, the comfortable, and the new without "razzle dazzle" or ostentatious luxury. In the homes I design, I mix dark with light, smooth with textured, and keep the furniture and accessories as simple as possible. I have found inspiration in the delicate eighteenth-century English classicism of the Adam brothers, as well as English-style cottages and the Georgian architecture of the American colonial period.

When putting the final touches on homes designed in this style, I love the moment when personal items collected over the years are put back carefully into each room. This ephemera, whether it's an old classic camera, a favorite book, or even miniature dollhouse furniture passed from one generation to the next, makes the space come alive. There is always a fine line between a collection and clutter, but a strong editorial eye keeps these homes balanced between austere and lived in.

Primary residences can be made to feel like vacation homes with the addition of those classic trappings of summers by the beach: playing cards, vintage poker chips, and beach reading.

LEFT Pool houses in particular should blur the line between the interior and exterior. The exterior structure virtually disappears when the folding glass doors are pulled back.

FOLLOWING PAGE, RIGHT This breakfast nook was designed with a family in mind. The chairs, which have been covered in vinyl making them quite durable, are decidedly nautical in theme and take their design from vintage life preservers.

keeping it real

THE ROOMS IN beach classic homes may have nautical references or may be simply crafted with nautical precision, but there is always a vague feeling that the house wouldn't be harmed if it were to float away on a high tide. Wood and white dominate these interiors, as do classic American antiques, mixed with a few European pieces upholstered in simple, pure forms. White paneling, bead board, and tongue and groove are the rule, not the exception. These homes are influenced by the proud austerity of the Shaker style, but—just as a Craftsman house is—they are built to last.

Though a beach classic home celebrates everyday living, avoid mass-produced items as much as possible. You can find great catalog furnishings and objects, but it's important to use some one-of-a-kind furniture and textiles. Catalogs are seasonal because such decor goes out of style. Original pieces have stayed in circulation for a reason. I always use vintage lighting when I can; these older items, especially in beach classic homes, give the room soul. Light linen curtains carry this aesthetic as easily as they carry the sea breezes.

A bowl of shells may sit on a coffee table and a surfboard may lean against a wall, but a priceless painting might hang over a couch where the family dog curls up every afternoon. Life is never too precious, and furnishings, or whole rooms for that matter, are never off-limits. The color palette is pale and neutral, yet rooms are flooded with natural light. Whether the home is used part-time or all of the time, it is always a family home—where warm feelings and relaxed elegance are the order of the day. It is an innately chic style that seems effortless and without self-consciousness. The beach classic house is peaceful, welcoming, simple, and clean, yet filled with energy and joy, all the architectural embodiments of the American Dream.

OPPOSITE Blown-glass elements, simple as they may be, provide extra sparkle to any room. I found these vintage pieces at a local antiques store that specializes in nautically inspired objects.

FOLLOWING PAGE Unlikely as it may be, this simple corner became a favorite resting spot for the owners of this classic home. The balance of color and form between the distressed leather chair and the fine antique Oriental rug complete an aesthetic triangle, with the landscape painting as its peak.

classic colors: khakis and a white shirt

WHETHER A ROOM IS WHITE, so its walls are not even noticeable, or painted some shade of yellow, blue, or green, colors in beach classic homes must be chosen with restraint and care. There is a tendency, when people want a big change in the design of their home, to suggest some outlandish shade for a room or two. While I'm very much in support of bold design choices, I use the "pants metaphor" to make my point. Imagine if you were told that you could only wear one pair of pants for the rest of your life, day in and day out. A horrible thought, indeed. Now imagine that those pants were puce or cobalt blue. You might love them for the first few days, but you would eventually feel ridiculous and would become instantly sick of wearing them after a few weeks, to be sure. But if those same pants were khaki, you could probably stand it. So too with a room in your house: the general color scheme should probably (and I say "probably" because there are always exceptions to every design tenet) be neutral, with bold injections of color from pillows, accents, and accessories. Think of the backgrounds and upholstery as khakis and a white shirt; your pillows and accessories should act like a bright silk scarf, added for accent. You never want to be the loudest person at the party, and neither should the elements in your room.

Color schemes in the beach classic style are inspired by the weekend wardrobe. I use brick reds, indigo blues, and natural greens to bring the outside in. Seamless indoor/outdoor lifestyles are supported by rooms whose durable fabric and furnishings encourage everyday use. Simplicity is king here, and highly edited selections of furnishings and objects create a flow from one room to the next. These playful spaces may feature unexpected bursts of color and light—a peacock blue pillow on a cream denim upholstered sofa, for

OPPOSITE Though many rooms in this home are celebrations of prints, pattern, and color, the entrance hall is kept free of clutter, instead focusing on the sweeping architectural forms that are the soul of this home.

PREVIOUS PAGE, LEFT The addition of a collection of gleaming white shells not only counterbalances the darkness in this painting but also alludes to the ocean in an unexpected way.

PREVIOUS PAGE, RIGHT Upon closer scrutiny, the chandelier in this dining room features mismatched colored glass pendants that give the otherwise staid interior a bohemian flair, which is further enhanced by the curtains in an Indian-inspired print. The dining table is the classic addition to the design—a family heirloom. The custom-fabricated rolled mirror in the corner of the room has been split and separated with gold rosettes, allowing "liquid" golden light to bounce around the dining room, which bathes guests in the most flattering of hues.

example—but the overall effect of these American spaces is one of freedom and light.

Early American interiors were often red, scarlet red, in fact, and I love to use red in these types of homes. This pure American color suggests energy, spirit, power, and love. I also use sage green and gray-green, both inspired by the colors of coastal grasses. Earth brown, grass, sea, and sky are colors that never go out of fashion, namely because they are found in the natural world and are therefore familiar and comforting. Despite these tones' ubiquity, they can still feel fresh when combined with rich, satisfying natural textures and loose weaves in natural shades.

Walls are painted in a subtle tone-on-tone palette. Plaster walls painted flat with semigloss wood work well. Paneling, tongue and groove, and bead board walls are painted with a slight sheen. Wallpaper often features woven textures or stripes so the more traditional patterns feel modern.

Inspired by the precision that is Nantucket, this beamed ceiling features plaster instead of the normal board and batten, giving the space a cleaner, crisper feeling. Though highly formal at first glance, every surface and piece of furniture in this living room invites use.

lasting worth, timeless quality

BEACH CLASSIC FLOORS are wood in tones of toffee, polished oak, or warm walnut that anchor the white walls and woodwork and warm up interiors. If the wood is painted, it is almost always white.

Brick is used on floors and fireplace surrounds, but stone is kept to a minimum. Bathroom countertops are done in dark brown veined marble or traditional white honed Carrara marble.

Pure classic shapes with tailored slipcovers dominate the furniture style, as in a summer house. You might find painted American stick wicker furniture on the back porch and, in the bedrooms, cannonball beds in dark stains and pencil-post beds without testers.

Mixing pattern, line, and color is sometimes risky when not addressed properly. In beach classic homes, seemingly disparate styles often work in harmony with one another when the base colors, the size and shape of the lines, or the general historical and cultural aesthetics are similar. Finding this balance can be as easy as layering materials together before decisions are made, or as difficult as installing them in the room and stepping back before making a permanent choice.

I love woven and cotton rugs for these homes. Originally used in nineteenth-century America as an inexpensive alternative to Oriental rugs, these are easy to take care of and look great. Back then, Shaker, Amish, and Pennsylvania weavers worked on handlooms to create strong, practical, and straightforward work that fits in easily with beach classic style. Antique Indian rugs are another option in these environments because of their allover patterns and earthy tones—they are flattering, more durable, and feel less precious than more expensive Oriental rugs. They also serve as a great foundation to the beach classic color schemes.

Given the right amount of square footage, a bathroom can function like a lounge.

Incorporating old and new, prints and patterns, and surfaces of both wood and metal makes a room come alive.

beachwood

IN MANY WAYS, Beachwood is the epitome of the Southern California beach house, but with a nod to the East Coast. Though its scale is large, the home was deliberately designed to feel as if it had organically expanded over time, as if each section were added as the needs of the family grew from one generation to the next. The house may be large, but it never feels overwhelming or ostentatious. It is scaled for today's way of living but finds its roots in the best of the past.

I looked east, in part, for this most western of homes. It may seem counterintuitive, but those classic beach homes along the Eastern Seaboard provided some of the most pointed references. The weathered, sea-battered vacation homes of Cape Cod, East Hampton, and Maine were built to last, and for centuries have withstood brutal weather. As a result, these homes project a sense of history and place that feel distinctly American and instantly inspire an intangible comfort. Moreover, it is from these houses on the East Coast that Southern California beach architecture finds its inspiration. One need only venture just a few blocks from the beach in Santa Monica, California, to find incredible turn-of-the-century beach homes that look as if they were transported from Nantucket Sound.

The front door and entrance hall of Beachwood typify this experience: you'll find contrasting materials as you walk into the home, from painted white siding to cream plaster, that give the home the feel of having been a tiny beach shack that grew and expanded over time. And though the home has a decidedly East Coast feeling, the addition of teak casings on all windows and doors is a nod to the homes of Hawaii and the Pacific Rim aesthetic.

This house was designed for a party—two parties, actually. This couple wanted a second home situated on their favorite beach where they could hold a fête twice a year that is the stuff of legends. Unlike many homes, where the primary function might be slightly less defined, this is a home built for entertaining. As such, it required rooms of a particular scale, coupled with places for a large group to relax, sleep, and communally dine. The master bedroom, traditionally

The alternating geometry of the Ipe wood deck, the round teak bench, and the railing creates a visual feast that never ceases to delight the eye.

placed in the "best" location in a house, is set back a bit from the beach and is neither the biggest room nor the room with the best views. Beach houses are not meant for squirreling away in your bedroom all day but are communal experiences intended for sharing with friends and family. The master bedroom is for sleeping and remains a simple, functional space.

The best views in this house are actually from the second floor deck, where the most sweeping panoramas are maximized. We designed the deck so people can easily congregate here. It also happens to be the location of the hot tub, which sees high traffic.

The main entertaining rooms, including the living and family rooms, have been specifically designed for parties and feature open, flowing transitions from one space to the next. The floors, most done in a wide plank, are built above padded subfloors of the same material and design as that of professional ballet studios. This unexpected detail gives the rooms a subtle, ebullient feel as guests lightly bounce from room to room, often to the beat of DJ music played at events.

The kitchen and family rooms, located on the second floor, are in fact separated by a large opening in a shared wall, but are visually connected so that activity in both rooms remains in tandem. This same opening also allows for a gorgeous ocean view from both rooms. The kitchen itself was designed with this same feeling of heritage. The stove and refrigerator are mounted just slightly farther out than the built-in cabinetry, which is set in at the standard twenty-four inches, providing the room some visual relief from the monotony that can result from entirely flush cabinetry. The mismatched hardware, including the drawer pulls and the plumbing fixtures, further the look of a space that has evolved over time.

The levels of the home were designed with the idea of layers in mind, each with a relationship to the natural environment. The top floor is almost all bedrooms, whose primary view is the sky. As such, the color palette is pale and subdued. The middle layer relates to the earth and water—and here one can see the lawn just outside

The many bedrooms for out-of-town guests are each filled with comfortable essentials for an overnight stay. However, we purposely did not equip them with minibars and refrigerators to avoid that hotel-like feeling so many large houses have, and to encourage guests to linger in the more communal areas instead.

the doors. The lower level has views of sand and is the location for entertaining, so the colors are more saturated than in the rest of the house. This level features navy, teal, and orange as the primary accents—colors much more durable for high-traffic environments. The sand view is also rather harsh and highly reflective, and these deeper colors absorb some of those effects, making it easier to feel relaxed in the room.

I filled the home with collections of things that add to the sense of history. There are American tables, European chairs, pieces in bamboo and wicker, and simple, rustic country pieces. Plank tables, used a number of times in this home, look better as they age, and you can set drinks on them without worry. I chose furniture that wasn't intended to be serious or luxurious as much as comfortable.

One of the most arresting features of this house is the center stair hall that serves as the key element of the house. The scale of a three-story staircase of this nature can often make it feel cold and lacking compared to the rest of the home. To counteract this effect, I had the space wallpapered in a warm raffia that gave the staircase a closed-in, more whimsical feel, providing a great backdrop for hanging art and photography. We gathered together a collection of ocean- and beach-related paintings and images in non-matching frames and mats and hung them under brass picture lamps. The art spirals up the walls and lends life to an otherwise anonymous transition.

Above all, this is a casual home. Though the size can be imposing, the rooms have been designed to a manageable scale that encourages interaction and relaxed living. The furniture features the most classic shapes and has been covered in natural materials with bits of pattern and color for visual punctuation. This understated aesthetic gives the house a feeling that it is summer all year round: you never feel uncomfortable lounging in your swimsuit here.

OPPOSITE To achieve the beach classic look, mixtures of high and low, important and found, well known and obscure create collections that are familiar, deliberate, and always pleasing to the eye.

FOLLOWING PAGE, LEFT Small river stones add a natural element to this bathroom.

FOLLOWING PAGE, RIGHT This custom-designed dining room table is built entirely of reclaimed wood. Building new pieces with old materials is a way to give rooms the feeling of history.

The pale blue glazed tile adds texture and mottled light to this kitchen.

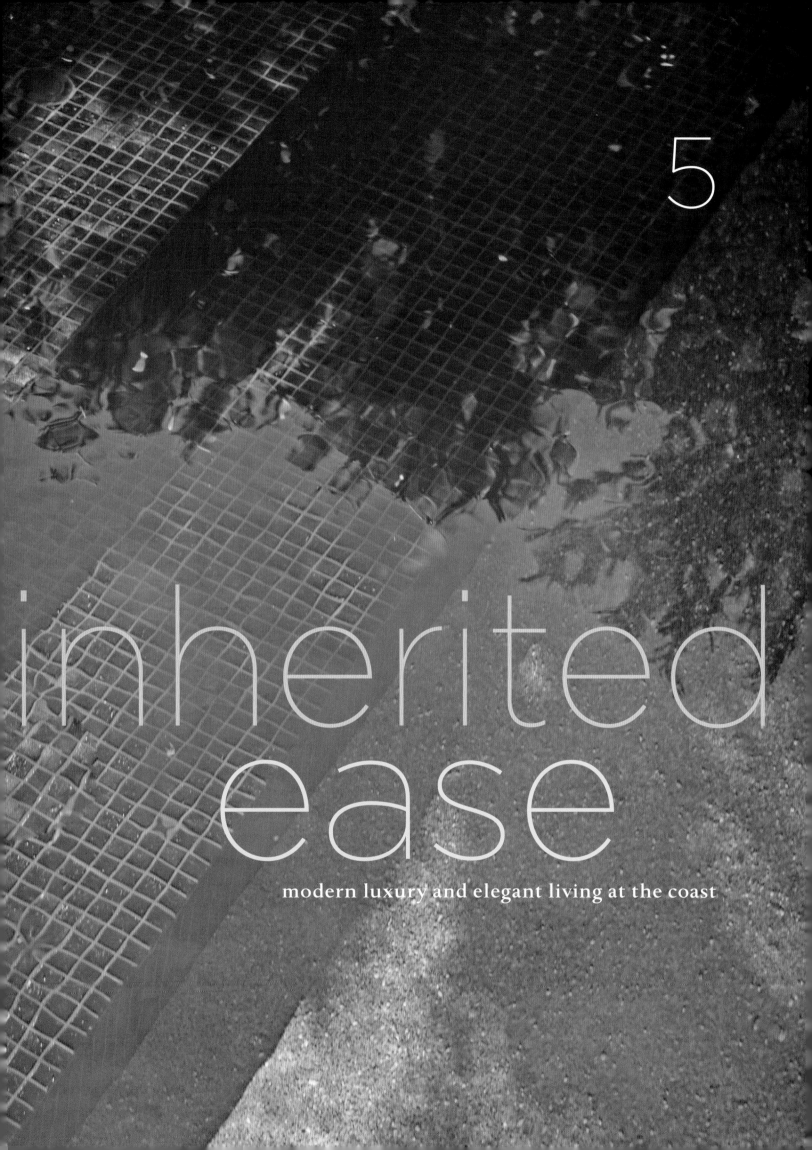

inherited ease

modern luxury and elegant living at the coast

LIKE A BESPOKE SUIT OR A HANDMADE automobile, true luxury is timeless and lasting and transcends fashion and trends. It's an ease that feels "inherited," if you will—a mixture of furnishings, color, and objects made from materials meant to last, not just through next season, but through generations. Platinum bathtubs, crocodile upholstery, and custom-designed silk wall treatments might be paired with seventeenth-century French upholstered pieces and hand-knotted silk rugs to create a concert of grace and harmony that is both comfortable and entirely chic. These are coastal homes of the highest quality and style, with more formality than you might imagine other beach houses to have.

comfort and luxury,
grace and balance

WE DECORATE OUR HOMES because we care about supporting a life well lived. I became a decorator to help people find that elusive balance between comfort and luxury, and to help the people I design for discover who they are by the way that they want to live in their home. Comfort and luxury are at the heart of coastal living and go hand in hand with style, grace, and balance. A coastal modern home is not meant to elicit jealousy in others, to impress someone who walks in the door for the first time, or to show how much the owner has. A home should reflect and support how you see yourself in both your public and your private lives: communal rooms, like the living and dining rooms, are always very different from those private spaces where guests shouldn't linger. Past, present, and future intersect in a well-designed residence.

The homes that I've designed and call inherited ease are reflections of this design philosophy: great classic pieces mix freely with objects and furnishings from many eras, yet each piece, each pattern, and every texture is at once timeless and lasting and therefore completely modern. There is always an honesty to the materials, furnishings, and details in my inherited ease homes, and each choice reflects the belief that it is the details themselves that create life and beauty in a home.

I choose new unlacquered brass fixtures that will age gently over those that have been treated with a chemical patina, and I finish hardwood floors and fine wood details with natural oils rather than with harsh plastic chemical varnishes and lacquers. I wax floors with natural rather than artificial products, not because it's ethical (though that is a benefit), but because natural materials and finishes add a visceral, human quality to interior spaces.

OPPOSITE Though everything in this house was purchased specifically for the project, each piece was chosen because it feels as though it has been passed down through generations of a single family.

PREVIOUS PAGES Bursts of color draw the eye and highlight themes like well-placed punctuation marks.

the patience for age

I OFTEN ENCOUNTER HOMES that simply feel wrong. They may be large, brand new, and very pretty to look at, but there is a coldness and artificiality to the design. Inherited ease aims to counteract this. A person may feel inclined to choose artificially aged brass doorknobs, for example, because they have that "old" look that some equate with sophistication and "good design." Instead, details like this give residences a vulgar, tract-home look that is the clichéd nouveau riche style in which almost no one feels entirely comfortable. Instead, it's best to choose details and finishes that age naturally.

Ours is a world that celebrates speed and has no patience for age. It's time we celebrated the wisdom and knowledge that comes with life experience, both in terms of homes and people. This is the essence of inherited ease: it's a mix of high and low, old and new, classic and contemporary, yet all pieces work together in a balanced and highly layered concert of comfort and design that carries history in its bones, and with that history comes weight and integrity.

A great way to understand how inherited ease works is by the example of the rug. Many homeowners obsess about its role; they think about how that rug will match and "anchor" the room, how it will interact with the furnishings and window treatments, or how it will either catch the eye or fade away. They are always surprised when I tell them that though the rug may be the anchor to the room, it is often the last layer to go in. Yes, rugs should pick up colors and patterns utilized in the space, but a rug should never match or look like it was used to set a design scheme for an interior space. In the inherited ease aesthetic, your furnishings, objects, inherited furnishings, and any new purchases should work together. But they should never appear as if they were part of some elaborately planned room that looks more like an event than a timeless space.

Personal collections of unusual objects are key to creating a home that reflects who you are.

Think of your spaces as you might a family holiday party; it is the rare family in which all members "match." Everyone is his or her own person, with different tastes, hopes, dreams, and personalities—that is how a family should be. When you get everyone together, there may be some dramatic moments, but somehow it all just works, because there is a common thread that binds these lives, and so too should it be with a room.

Design, especially interior design, can become too precious and take on a staged look. Rooms where everything is placed "just so" are appealing in the same way that a photograph in a magazine draws you in: they're fun to look at, to daydream about, perhaps to critique, but not suited to the reality of everyday life. Remember that even elegant rooms get used—which is the point, and evidence, of their success.

This magnificent view inspired a home's aesthetic: one that's meant to draw the eye to the vast, ever-changing sea.

Red accents, like crimson lipstick on a lovely face, provide graphic contrast in this neutral, masculine space. The vintage fabrics and hides give the room an inherited aesthetic.

the well-layered room

THE SUCCESS OF A ROOM is in the layers, and you can never
have enough of them. This may sound counterintuitive, as "busy"
rooms are the enemy of good taste, but busy and layered are very
different. Layered rooms are balanced, harmonious, and easy to
live in. Busy rooms are chaotic and messy and push people away.
Layering doesn't work if everything you place in the room is from
the same store, in the same color family, from the same period, or
is just a mixture of unrelated objects, patterns, and furnishings that
are thrown together in the hopes that they work when piled up like
puppies on a postcard.

Think of a well-layered room like this: structure first,
accessories last. Start by choosing the floor (preferably something in
a hardwood), the wall treatments, the paint, the ceiling treatment
and color, and, finally, the overhead lighting. Choose upholstered
furniture, end tables, coffee tables, high-wall furniture, and low-wall
furniture. Once this structure is in place, start adding layers: pillows,
throws, books, and accessories. The larger the home, the more square
footage in your room, the more layers you need. Though the line
between clutter and balance is thin indeed, use your instincts when
adding design elements to your rooms. Because there are no hard-
and-fast rules when it comes to creating a space that is unfussy, clean,
appealing, and, most important, reflects your style, don't be afraid of
adding too many things when you first begin arranging your objects
and furnishings. Don't choose things because they match—try
everything. Editing is almost as important as layering, and you can
always take things out after putting them in.

A bedroom should be a cocoon,
a womb, a jewel box; protected
from light and sound, the room
should embrace you the moment
you walk in. The gray flannel glued
to the wall like wallpaper, absorbs
both light and sound, creating a
peaceful environment where senses
are subtly muted.

RIGHT This tablescape is typical of the rest of this home: opulent, passionate, and entirely reflective of the owner's tastes and lifestyle.

FOLLOWING PAGE, LEFT Nothing is more luxurious than knowledge.

FOLLOWING PAGE, RIGHT Even this breakfast table is a study in elegant living.

the modernity of inherited ease

THOUGH LIVING ROOMS or bedrooms might come to mind when you think of inherited ease, the entire home embodies this comfortably elegant design style. Kitchens, for example, might be entirely white tile, with fixtures, dishware, and window treatments in styles that connote early-twentieth-century sensibilities shaped by the streamlined modernity of the burgeoning Industrial Revolution. Yet over the deep double sinks might hang two French-inspired chandeliers that one would expect in a fashionable boudoir. Though these styles sound like unexpected juxtapositions, the clean lines and color of the disparate elements work together in a concert of line and form.

What makes these rooms modern is the way these antiques and vintage-inspired furnishings and objects are arranged in a room. Different periods and styles are used with an eye toward their relation to their use and "place" among the other pieces in each space. Two pieces that don't readily seem to match will suddenly be made more beautiful by the casual way they are situated together. No one object or piece of furniture is treated as more precious than another.

Traditional pieces of furniture are arranged in a modern way, making these rooms welcoming to anyone who enters. There is an ease to inherited materials—whether you acquire them through ancestry or from the flea market—due to their care-worn history that is at the essence of the coastal modern lifestyle. Rooms in inherited ease homes are useful and livable. They bring the formal design elements of the past into today's more casual lifestyle without sacrificing any beauty, and the sustainability of found and inherited objects pleases our modern, eco-friendly sensibilities. Inherited ease is romantic and playful, but practical. It allows us to celebrate our stories or to create new histories—and what could be more modern than that?

The essence of inherited ease is in the layering. Nothing looks piled up, yet there are many objects, each with its proper place. This library features hand-oiled bookshelves, an antique chair covered with zebra hide, and a custom Chinese vessel lamp.

the ridges

THE RIDGES is a house like none other I have designed. Created from the finest materials, it was almost entirely handcrafted. The home positively glitters with bespoke elements, which imbue it with the feel of a rare, private European residence, kept in a well-appointed family for generations. Unlike many of my beach home designs, this house is not meant to be overtly "relaxed" or "beachy." Stepping into this home is akin to spending an evening in one of the finer family-owned residences of Paris, where beauty and lasting craftsmanship are more important than fashion and trend. But unlike large apartments and townhouses in cities like Paris and London, this is a one-story home in a very warm place. Consequently, we added a plethora of connections to the outdoors, including many pocketing sets of French doors, big windows, and breezy passageways that are more typical of a coastal home.

Details like doorknobs of pure silver, a bathtub plated in platinum, and plaster walls that have been lovingly hand-burnished create a remarkable hideaway. This couple came to me looking for a house that was, above all, completely personal and entirely unique—a paean to beauty and luxury without compromise. The homeowners, who have multiple residences, wanted the house to evoke a classic European townhouse whose furnishings and design had been acquired over time, from generations of family and friends. Nothing in the home could feel "decorated," yet it all had to work as one cohesive design scheme.

It is always a challenge finding ways to make interiors appear as though they have organically grown over time. Far too often, professionally designed homes take on a stiff, decorated look. As we were shopping for this home, we made a point to look for pieces we thought were attractive, and we focused on how they might fit in with the rest of the collection later. The objects came first, even before the furnishings or color schemes were considered.

Objects were chosen for their singular beauty, but never for their relationship to anything else purchased or made for the home.

The backyard at The Ridges was designed to function as a seamless extension of the interior spaces. There are no rules when it comes to your outdoor spaces: even exterior furnishings can be refined, sleek, and modern.

By following this unique guiding principle, the home manages to seem at once lived-in and personal, and beyond luxurious.

This young couple was looking for a home that felt formal, urban, and sophisticated. Furnishings, fabrics, and color were selected not for their durability, but rather for quality and craftsmanship. The couple had no children, so the need for easily washable surfaces, bright colors, and multiple child-centric bedrooms was moot. Instead, the home is a tribute to a more structured way of living, and there was never a question of whether a material or a piece of furniture was too precious or too fragile. Very rich and dark, the home makes ample use of blacks, both matte and shiny, and darker shades of green and gray.

Because the home is situated in a very sunny and warm climate, we chose materials for either their reflective or their absorptive qualities. Every corner, no matter the level of use, contains something lovely, unique, and often custom-fabricated for this house. Even the kitchen, which is perhaps the lightest room in the house, features a pair of gorgeous silver chandeliers hanging over the center island.

Like any dramatic home, the front door and entrance hall set the stage for the experience of this home. The front door is unmistakably massive, made of very deep rich ebonized walnut and punctuated with a custom-made oversized doorknob of pure silver. Once you enter the first hall, you are surrounded by Fortuny fabric covering the walls and a pair of antique frame benches that have been upholstered in custom hand-cut velvet in a tiger stripe from Clarence House. To offset the luxury so the space doesn't feel too Versailles-like, and to add some modernity, we hung black-and-white photography on the walls.

As you leave the entrance hall, you see that the living room and the library are joined as one larger room, but they can be separated by giant mahogany pocket doors that stay hidden most of the time. In contrast to most houses I design, the furniture is laid out as you might find in a gentlemen's club. Rather than the typical sofa setup, four

This couple is very social and wanted spaces throughout the home that felt lived-in, luxurious, and inviting. The intimacy of this sitting room, which centers around an efficient convertible coffee table whose sections conveniently pull out, is enhanced by the omission of any couches. These sumptuous club chairs encourage conversation.

wing chairs surround a coffee table. The floor is covered in a densely jewel-toned antique carpet.

The library is filled with books and objects that relate to the various passions enjoyed by this interesting couple, who share most things, including work. The two are often found in this room sitting at the large writing table, which is flanked by two gilded chairs covered in antique zebra skin. The room feels exotic and lived-in compared with most home offices. It's an inspiring place to work.

Adjacent to the library is a fully stocked bar and the formal dining room, both designed for a decidedly adult style of entertaining—there are no high chair stools at the ready here. The dining room is centered around a custom table created from salvaged wood and surrounded by chairs that we covered in dark green silk. The legs are gilded platinum, the chandelier antique crystal. When the lights are dimmed and candles are lit, these two rooms take on a mysterious, twinkling glow that is the epitome of the way this home enchants.

In a residence of this exquisite quality and with such attention to detail, the walls and ceilings present a canvas for artisans of many sorts to work their handcrafted magic. The walls throughout the home are burnished plaster in a pewterlike shade, giving the rooms the effect of being constantly bathed in candlelight. The ceiling in the library is coffered in richly oiled mahogany, a lovely foil to the flatten-panel detail of the stained mahogany ceiling in the dining room.

In stark contrast to the brooding, clublike tones of the library and dining rooms, the family room, the breakfast room, and the kitchen are in a decidedly lighter spectrum. These rooms get more natural illumination, have more connection to the exterior, and are intended for use during the day. The plaster is the same color as the other rooms, but the furniture is black, white, and gray so these daytime spaces can keep with the sophistication of the rest of the home.

A small door near the shower leads to a private garden that the couple often enjoys.

LEFT In the master bathroom, we created a unique feature: a bathroom within a bathroom for the woman of the house. The walls are covered in silver leaf, and the bathtub is plated in platinum. The drapes are of the finest tropical wool, tailored to fall like an Armani suit.

FOLLOWING PAGE, LEFT Passion—for life, love, even shoes—should be celebrated in the home.

FOLLOWING PAGE, RIGHT Classic design, whether it's found in a residence or a handbag, is timeless and can serve as decoration.

6

native woods

warmth and comfort at the ocean's edge

ONCE YOU'VE BEGUN TO IMMERSE
yourself in your home's natural environment,
observing the surrounding colors, patterns,
textures, forms, and lines, you'll be able to
visualize the important elements for your
home.

Natural materials are a powerful way
to connect a home to its location. Whenever
possible I use wood, stone, sand, water, and
weathered glass throughout a residence
because these materials imbue a project with
life in a way nothing else can. Elements drawn
from nature produce a calm atmosphere
that can be enriched by varying textures and
shades of indigo, black, and gray.

MY NATIVE WOODS homes, which embody a number of different architectural and interior styles, are literally filled with wood and wooden accents, and they invite a healthy, natural life. Native woods homes find inspiration in the gorgeous, open-plan tropical homes in places like Bali, Hawaii, and Brazil, where the separation between the interior and exterior is sometimes nonexistent. Residences in these locations often feature walls that completely fold away, and they incorporate materials readily found in the surrounding regions, namely those rare tropical hardwoods that delight the senses. Their expansive, welcoming designs embrace the natural world.

Native woods is the purest of coastal modern styles. When you immerse yourself in the splendor of the ocean and watch as the sun sets at the horizon, it is impossible not to be moved by the grand simplicity of it all. Just as bits of washed-up beach glass reflect the world around them, so too do native woods homes.

In designing these interiors, I make an effort to address the four elements found in nature: water, earth, air, and fire. For example, when addressing water, you may have the luxury of an ocean view to celebrate, or you can add a restrained pond or fountain that is tucked away in the garden. Air is addressed simply by the wind gently blowing the fronds of a palm outside a window. Earth can be referenced with a grass rug or in the walls whose colors find inspiration in the surrounding environs—earth-based color schemes and natural plaster walls. Finally, fire elements are present in beautifully realized fireplaces, fire pits, or the use of candles and torches. All of these elements together create harmony, balance, and an intangible sense of order and calm that only comes when the four forces of nature are in tune with one another.

OPPOSITE This native woods home typifies the Japanese aesthetic. The pea gravel entrance was designed to evoke a Zen-like experience as one enters the property. The beam trellis in oiled hardwood further blurs the line between the indoor and outdoor spaces.

OPENING PAGE The cast-iron stove provides a visual anchor in this space. The daybed in a simple faded Suzani print is a welcome perch for getting a bit of afternoon sun.

PREVIOUS PAGES The deck at Bien Sur evokes the magic of this coastal wonderland. Earth, air, fire, and water come together to create an experience where the lines between the natural world and the built environment are nonexistent.

FOLLOWING PAGE, LEFT This moment reminds me of an aquarium. The specimen stone provides a waterlike backdrop to these sea-inspired objects.

FOLLOWING PAGE, RIGHT The rectangular window above the bed surrounds and invites nature without sacrificing privacy.

using wood in the home

DESIGN ELEMENTS like wide plank flooring in teak or mahogany; stained wooden beams exposed to the elements; rough-hewn ceramics; and rugs, walls, and furnishings in colors that reflect the natural world join in concert with furnishings built from gorgeous hardwoods of all types. I often use simple farm-style tables along with well-worn accessories that are softened by comfortable sofas and chairs, all covered in natural linen.

If you've ever been lucky enough to spend time in a great beach house, one of the most overlooked yet integral parts of its success is the mix of old and new, especially in the furnishings and the building materials. Salty air is harsh and corrosive, and anyone who has left deck chairs outside at the beach long enough knows that the combination of sun and salt does to untreated wood what it does to hair—bleaches it and dries it out. There is a beach patina that simply cannot be faked. Even the richest, darkest woods, the thickest coatings of exterior paint, or shellacked furniture will eventually succumb to the power of the sea.

Once I realized that the essence of coastal modern lies, in part, in these well-worn materials, rich colors, and strong pieces that carry history in their bones, I began to translate this into my inland native woods homes in order to connect them to an imagined coast. These homes are designed using building materials rooted in nature (wood, stone, shells), coupled with personal objects and furnishings that evoke a sense of place and history linked with both nature and the style of architecture and the culture in which the home sits. My native woods homes often feel at once vaguely Asian and contemporary, but always comfortable, relaxed, and elegant—as all homes (and hostesses, for that matter) should be.

Beauty at its most simple: the vintage coral and antique brass shark find a home on this live-edge coffee table.

LEFT Beauty and functionality go
hand in hand.

FOLLOWING PAGES A view to inspire.

To create the look and feel of a Balinese pavilion, the original ceilings were blown out to reveal the peak underneath, which I then covered in a Douglas fir stained to resemble teak.

finding inspiration
from exotic locales

THE PRINCIPAL IDEA of native woods—think locally while keeping a global perspective—really nods its head to coastal modern style. The very essence of native woods style was born in far-flung locales like Australia, Indonesia, and Sri Lanka. Exquisite and rare tropical hardwoods like Makassar ebony, rosewood, and ironwood are used liberally to complement the interior color schemes and to create an intimate interplay between the indoor and outdoor spaces. Interior spaces in these exotic locales are often soaring, open plans in which large banks of sliding doors and windows can be opened to eliminate the separation between inside and out. Fabric accents are often simple, plain colors: using manmade patterns on fabrics and walls would only distract from what nature has already done so well—sometimes the pattern of the wood grain is more than enough. When utilizing tropical hardwoods, or wood of any kind, use reclaimed or recycled product when possible. Not only is this vital in preserving the earth's forests, but these "used" woods carry a patina that is unmatched in new woods.

Native woods homes are studies in contemporary luxury: carefully chosen objects and furnishings imbue them with life, yet they are clean and modern and reflect the history of both the locale and the family that lives in the home. The feeling of walking into a native woods home is decidedly different from the experience of first entering a traditional coastal home. Darker accents and the liberal use of wood create a warmth and a comfort that cannot be duplicated. Rich textures, including stone, tile, and ceramic, add to this deeply visceral design experience.

Modern design is a celebration of unadorned clean lines and form, and there is nothing more basic or more "clean" than wood. Taking cues from Japanese design, this simple, pure space is pared down to its most essential elements so that what remains becomes poignant and powerful.

ABOVE These German ceramics look as if they came from Hawaii, and when coupled with this Japanese glass fisherman's float, the grouping takes on a vintage nautical feel that is at once unexpected and warm.

RIGHT To create separation, this quintessential outdoor room features dark wood offset by bold, acid colors in the upholstery and the rug, a reed ceiling, and thick foliage planted around the perimeter of the space.

nature takes
center stage

I HAVE FOUND inspiration in the smallest of places: I love smooth, matte seashells and weathered beach detritus, the pitted edge of a barnacle, or the live edge—where the rough-hewn edges are left exposed—of a piece of wood. In the same way that the beach naturally "edits" itself of extraneous objects through weather or the tides, native woods homes must be carefully edited of unnecessary furnishings and decoration so nature itself can take center stage. In the same vein, lighting should come from natural sources—via skylights, reflective surfaces, or table lamps and floor lamps rather than overhead lighting.

The colors are orange-based, ranging from terra-cotta to sienna; to maple syrup and molasses; to honey and clove—coupled with mellow tones of earth, wood, and fire. Indigo blues, teals, or sage greens are mixed in to intensify the experience. These earthy hues change the very quality of the light in the room and as such return a rich and earthy glow.

Floors, when not laid bare, are covered in rugs made of braided abaca dyed in deep teal, or of natural jute and paper. Antique carpets are powerful accents; Chinese antique rugs in strong oranges, blues, and golden yellows create a visual feast for the eye. Terra-cotta pavers make for wonderful floors; the smooth surfaces when stained a chocolate or charcoal provide a moody foundation to the orange tones of the tropical hardwoods used in these homes.

Native woods walls are either naturally oiled wood paneling in cedar or mahogany or plastered and pigmented in smooth mocha tones. The furnishings are simple antiques, including farm tables. Wood-framed chairs are best when made from exotic woods like coconut or afromosia. I also love Asian antiques, tansu chests, old altars, and furniture with upholstered blocked shapes in chunky linen fabrics.

The blue stone fireplace, the optical photograph, and the mahogany and nickel coffee table create a shiplike feeling that interacts visually with the highly textured rug and rattan light fixture hanging above the central table.

On the coffee table:

SANTA MONICA BEACH

ADVENTURES WITH OLD HOUSES

PINTURAS DE ANTONIO ALVAREZ DE GENULCOS

RIGHT Native woods interiors celebrate the beauty of surfaces in their natural state. This is wood simply being wood; the purity of these materials creates harmony.

FOLLOWING PAGE, LEFT The small breakfast nook, which worked nicely with the open floor plan, is flanked by a large painting whose dark wood grain reminded me of several rough-hewn wooden pieces used throughout the residence. While color is important when choosing art, in the sense that you have to live with it and love it, an art piece should speak to you. Remember that taste is subjective, and no one has the right answer when it comes to choosing the art that goes into your home. Follow your heart.

FOLLOWING PAGE, RIGHT This home is a paean to place: the fireplace is of locally culled jadestone, and the whale bone was found on the beach below. The ikat print fabric on an ottoman hints at a subtle tribal motif.

bien sur

THERE ARE FEW coastline locations that are as all encompassing as that of Big Sur, California. Situated on miles of craggy, windswept, forested coastline in Northern California, this home is unique in that it is the only one in such close proximity to the beach in all of Big Sur. As such, this project was as much about restraint as it was about cohesive design.

The home, named Bien Sur by the owners, was built in the '70s, and is classic Northern California hippy modern. Its redwood-and-glass aesthetic is distinct and yet pays timeless homage to a lifestyle that is as native as the thousand-year-old redwood forests that stretch from the rocky mountain peaks right down to the surf. It is an area of uncompromised beauty, and this home was quite an exciting project to approach.

The home itself needed no new construction, as the design was something that should not be touched, though the furnishings and color scheme needed some work. Originally done in a pale and yellow color scheme, the interior was distracting and incongruous. After spending many days enjoying the home and experiencing the sheer beauty of the area, I began to realize that I have only experienced this kind of raw natural power and beauty in one other place: Kauai, Hawaii. Much like those of the "Garden Isle," as Kauai is known, Big Sur's forests dramatically cascade straight to the beach, which often experiences brutal and relentless winds and rain. The landscape feels soaked in nature's sublime beauty.

I knew that I just needed to showcase this beauty through interiors that not only made sense for the space but also blended into the surrounding land. Those common issues that come up with most beach houses, namely issues related to entertaining, television placement, showcase furnishings, and interesting objects that might spark conversation, were not necessary here; nature is the ultimate entertainment center in a place like this.

The structure of this home, with its layers of cedar, redwood, and oak coupled with the exposed beams, made for a soaring, natural-

This home is designed to promote relaxation, reflection, and rest at every turn. The modular outdoor furniture can be moved into a variety of configurations to meet the needs of a constantly evolving social landscape.

feeling interior that required very little else than to get out of its way. The living room is surrounded in glass and sits under a giant skylight covered in a white, cloudlike curtain that can be pulled across to block out the harshest midday light.

Rather than paint the walls, we left the wood planks unfinished and raw. In the dining room and kitchen we stained the existing peach-toned terra-cotta floor to a deep charcoal to match the stained concrete floor of the living room. We placed a very chunky braided abaca rug dyed to a deep teal color that contrasts nicely with the constantly changing skies and the cedar plank walls and teak bookshelves.

The kitchen and dining area are completely open, forming one large room with no separation. Along the dining table there are two large window seats, a chunky ebonized daybed and a pair of Indonesian armchairs. This home is truly about everyone working together informally.

The bedrooms, located in a separate structure accessible only by walking outside, have a Zen-like quality. Decorated sparingly, the beds are upholstered in men's suiting fabric in deep charcoal herringbone and black pinstriping. The walls are cedar paneling, which gives the spaces a warm orange tone that is soothing and subtle.

Also located in a separate structure is the small artist's studio, in a wonderfully unfinished structure that was once used for storage. This incredible space, though small, features one of the best views in the home, as it is perched just at the edge of a soaring cliff. Heated by a cast-iron stove and entirely self-contained, this room—like the house itself—provides creative inspiration that feeds the soul and frees the mind.

OPPOSITE The large painting is like a window to another land.

FOLLOWING PAGE The living room at Bien Sur is among the most comfortable and inviting spaces in the home, drawing guests like a magnet. The large chair and couches are covered in chunky linen and surrounded by things that the owners love: books, art, and evidence of a life well lived.

LEFT AND FOLLOWING PAGE, LEFT
Vintage Pendleton camp blankets
and pillows are always at the ready
for guests who come to marvel at
the abundance of ocean life visible
in the surf below. Watching the
neighborhood sea otters play is a
favorite pastime of the locals.

FOLLOWING PAGE, RIGHT It's the
view that is the real focus in this
home. Everything, including the
rustic table and woven chairs, has
been chosen for its simplicity so
as not to distract from the ever-
changing natural wonders just
outside the sliding doors.

RESOURCES

There are many amazing shops, artisans, architects, and landscape designers that I value, and without them I would not be able to do what I do. The following is a highly edited list of some of my favorites. These are my go-to sources that I can always count on to achieve my coastal modern style.

FABRIC

Raoul Textiles
www.raoultextiles.com
Painterly, hand-printed linen fabrics

Le Gracieux
www.legracieux.com
Faded hand-blocked damasks, hand-screened prints, woven hemp

Anne Kirk Textiles
www.annekirktextiles.com
Wonderful washed, chunky linens

Rogers & Goffigon
www.delanyandlong.com
Solids, stripes, and textiles in subtle, muted palettes

PAINT

Farrow & Ball
www.farrow-ball.com
Matte paints with unsurpassed purity and depth of color

Pratt & Lambert
www.prattandlambert.com
The best faded neutrals and warm, washed grays

WALLCOVERING

Phillip Jeffries
www.phillipjeffries.com
Grasscloth, natural, woven, and textured wallcovering

SJW Studios
www.sjwstudios.com
Artisanal wallcovering in both texture and pattern

Caba Company
www.barkskin.com
Natural, sustainable "barkskin" for walls

WOOD FLOORS

Exquisite Surfaces
www.xsurfaces.com
Reclaimed antique French oak; modern European wide plank

Nikzad
www.nikzad.com
French white oak in a matte, unfinished looks

RUGS

Woodard & Greenstein
www.woodardweave.com
Striped cotton and wool area rugs in traditional American colors

Elizabeth Eakins
www.elizabetheakins.com
Hand-woven linen, wool, and cotton in muted palettes

Natural Carpet Co.
www.naturalcarpetcompany.com
Woven, seagrass, jute and abaca rugs

Dash & Albert
www.dashandalbert.com
Durable and affordable area rugs

International Flooring
www.dabbierifloorsinternational.com
Wall-to-wall carpets

Decorative Carpets
8900 Melrose Ave.
West Hollywood, CA 90069
310-859-6333
Great for custom area rugs

Mansour
8600 Melrose Ave.
West Hollywood, CA 90069
310-652-9999
Spectacular antique carpets and modern area rugs

Y&B Bolour
www.ybbolour.com
Wonderful, unusual antique carpets

BED LINENS

Nancy Koltes
www.nancykoltes.com
Classic, elegant, and timeless bedding

Matteo
www.matteohome.com
Garment-dyed linens with a vintage washed look

FURNISHINGS AND ACCESSORIES

Maison Au Naturel
www.maison819.net
Stylish selection of French rustic style; great pillows

Mecox Gardens
www.mecoxgardens.com
Hamptons-style new and vintage furniture and accessories

Big Daddy's Antiques
www.bdantiques.com
An eclectic collection of vintage and antique flea-market style

Lucca Antiques
www.luccaantiques.com
Italian, Spanish, and Belgian antique and reproduction furniture

Eccola
www.eccolaimports.com
Antique and vintage Italian furniture and lighting

Gibson Antiques
www.garygibson.com
A fascinating collection of antiques, eclectic accessories, and original artwork

Lawson-Fenning
www.lawsonfenning.com
Midcentury modern style

Lee Stanton Antiques
www.leestanton.com
Purveyor of fine period antiques

Antiques of the Sea
www.antiquesofthesea.com
A huge assortment of nautical antiques and collectibles

Blackman Cruz
www.blackmancruz.com
Extraordinary objects; rare, provocative, and eccentric

JF Chen
www.jfchen.com
A huge space filled with a wonderful mix of antiques in every period and style

Obsolete
www.obsoleteinc.com
Antiques, curiosities, and industrial artifacts

Hollyhock
www.hollyhockinc.com
Eighteenth- and nineteenth-century antiques mixed with home accessories and art

Downtown
www.downtown20.net
Original mix of distinctive twentieth-century design

Tower 20
www.timclarkedesign.com
Everything you need for the perfect beach house

Suzan Fellman
www.suzanfellman.com
Represents some of the most inventive textile designers and decorative art dealers in the world

Lief Antiques
www.liefalmont.com
The finest Gustavian antiques

Rooms and Gardens
www.roomsandgardens.com
Classical upholstered furniture, great pillows, and accessories

Tortoise
www.tortoiselife.com
A beautifully curated mix of Japanese accessories and functional objects

LIGHTING

Circa Lighting
www.circalighting.com
An extensive collection of reproduction lighting

Clate Grunden
www.clategrunden.com
Handmade parchment pendants and ceramic lamps

Remains
www.remains.com
Vintage and reproduction lamps

Paul Ferrante
www.paulferrante.com
Custom lighting; wonderful antiques

Reborn Antiques
http://www.rebornantiques.net
Custom lighting, indoor and out

Charles Edwards
www.charlesedwards.com
Beautifully detailed English lighting

Steven Handelman
www.stevenhandelmanstudios.com
Perfect lighting for seaside Mediterranean style

KITCHEN & BATH

Waterworks
www.waterworks.com
Best plumbing fixtures, both modern and traditional

Ann Sacks
www.annsacks.com
A wonderful selection of surfaces, tile, and stone

STONE & TILE

Mission Tile West
1227 Fifth St.
Santa Monica, CA 90401
310-434-9697
A great selection of reproduction historical tile

Heath Ceramics
www.heathceramics.com
Wonderful organic glazed tile

HARDWARE

Details Hardware
www.detailshardware.com
A great selection of modern hardware

Golden Lion
www.thegoldenlion.com
Beautiful French and Mediterranean options

Ashley Norton
www.ashleynorton.com
Great traditional oil-rubbed bronze pieces

Nanz
www.nanz.com
High-end, beautiful hardware

WINDOW COVERINGS

Drapery Work Room
1001 Tennessee St.
San Francisco, CA 94107
415-285-2344
Gorgeous hand-sewn draperies—the couture of curtains

Window Collections
www.windowcollections.com
Great for automated and motorized window coverings

Select Drapery
12213 Santa Monica Blvd.
Los Angeles, CA 90025
310-826-5600
Curtains, woven shades, and wood blinds

OUTDOOR

David Sutherland
www.davidsutherlandshowroom.com
Teak sofas and club chairs

Summit Furniture
www.summitfurniture.com
Great teak tables

Janus et Cie
www.janusetcie.com
Represents a wide array of outdoor furniture lines

ART/PHOTOGRAPHY

Leslie Sokolow
www.lesliesokolow.com
Moody beach and ocean shots

Grant Rohloff
www.grantrohloff.com
Vintage surf photography

Sears-Peyton Gallery
Macie Sherick
www.searspeyton.com
Represents amazingly talented artists and exhibits, many beach- and ocean-inspired works

ARCHITECTS

Tim Barber
www.timbarberltd.com
Sensitive, detailed, traditional architecture

KAA
www.kaadesigngroup.com
Styles ranging from traditional to tropical modern

Marmol Radziner
www.marmol-radziner.com
Midcentury restoration; organic modern

Michael Lee
www.mleearchitects.com
Beachy modern designs

Doug Burdge
www.buaia.com
The go-to architect for Malibu

LANDSCAPE

Art Luna Garden
www.artlunagarden.com
Formal yet free-flowing landscapes; available to work on both coasts

Andrea Cochran
www.acochran.com
Modern garden design; unmistakable sense of intimacy in scale and composition

Inner Gardens
www.innergardens.com
Great for indoor plants

The Tropics
7056 Santa Monica Blvd.
West Hollywood, CA 90038
323-469-1682
Exotic, rare, and unusual plants, indoor and out

Laurie Lewis
www.laurielewisdesign.com
Contextual landscapes that respond to the site, architect, and client

Jay Griffith
www.jaygriffith.com
Bold, expressive juxtapositions of materials, plants, and textures

THANK YOU to Will Speck, who came in to my store out of the blue and suggested that I do a book. A special thank-you to my literary agent, Jason Anthony, who believed in this project from the moment that Will introduced us—you truly made this happen.

Thank you to Clate Grunden—who has been with me since the beginning—and whose artistic vision and creativity is matched only by his patience. You keep my business running.

Thank you to Noah Webb, whose photographs brought my work to light, and whose aesthetic made this book so special.

Thank you to Jake Townsend for the beautiful words in this book, and for his patience and collaboration. You helped to make this book what it is.

Thank you to my incredibly creative staff at Tim Clarke Design: K. B. Kim, Anna Lobell, Alex Merin, and Stephen Sacks.

Thank you to KAA for creating the book proposal, my website, and consistently beautiful architecture projects.

Thank you to all of my wonderful clients, some of whose houses are pictured in the book and some whose are not. Without all of you I would not be able to do what I love to do.

A special thank-you to Merle and Peter Mullin.

Thank you to Manolo Langis, Natasha Harris, Nicholas Trikonis, and Surma Mauro: your creativity, support, and dedication are appreciated.

Thank you to art installers Katherine Leighnor and Jason David.

Thank you to C.R. Creative Services, who work tirelessly to install all my projects.

Last, but certainly not least, to this book's editor, Aliza Fogelson, to associate editor Angelin Borsics, and to everyone at Clarkson Potter: thank you for making this dream come true.